Fun with Mum

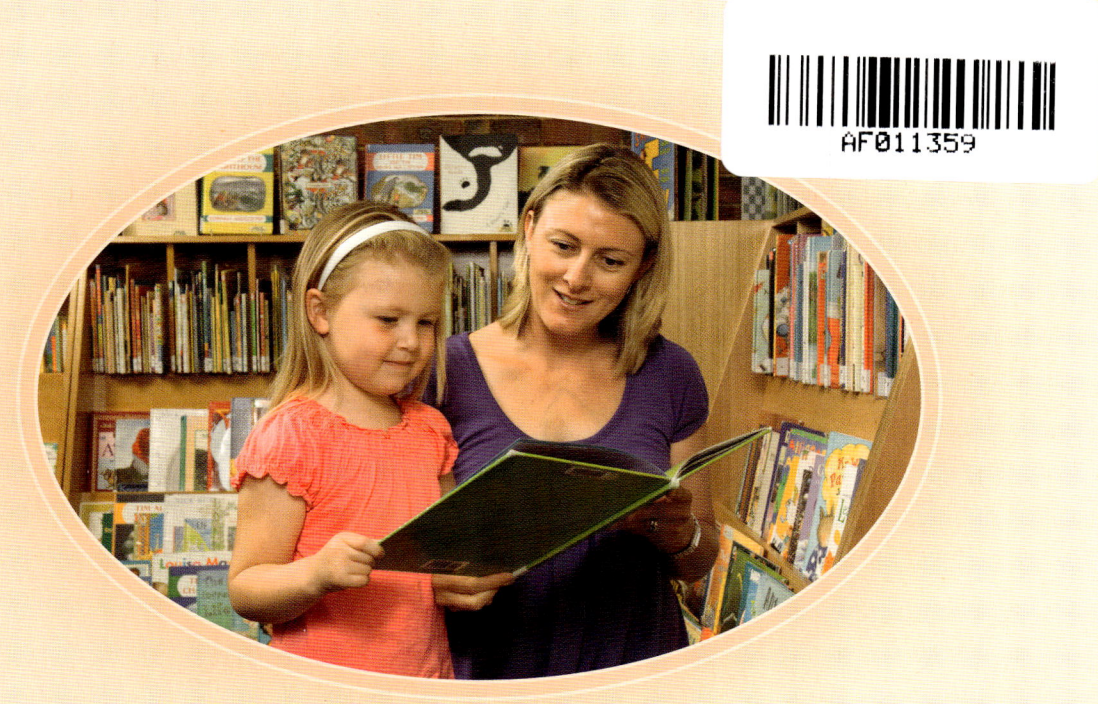

Mum and I
went to the park.

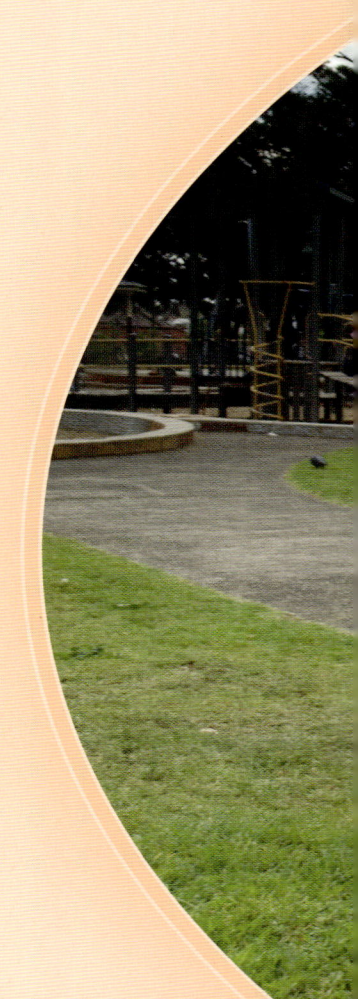

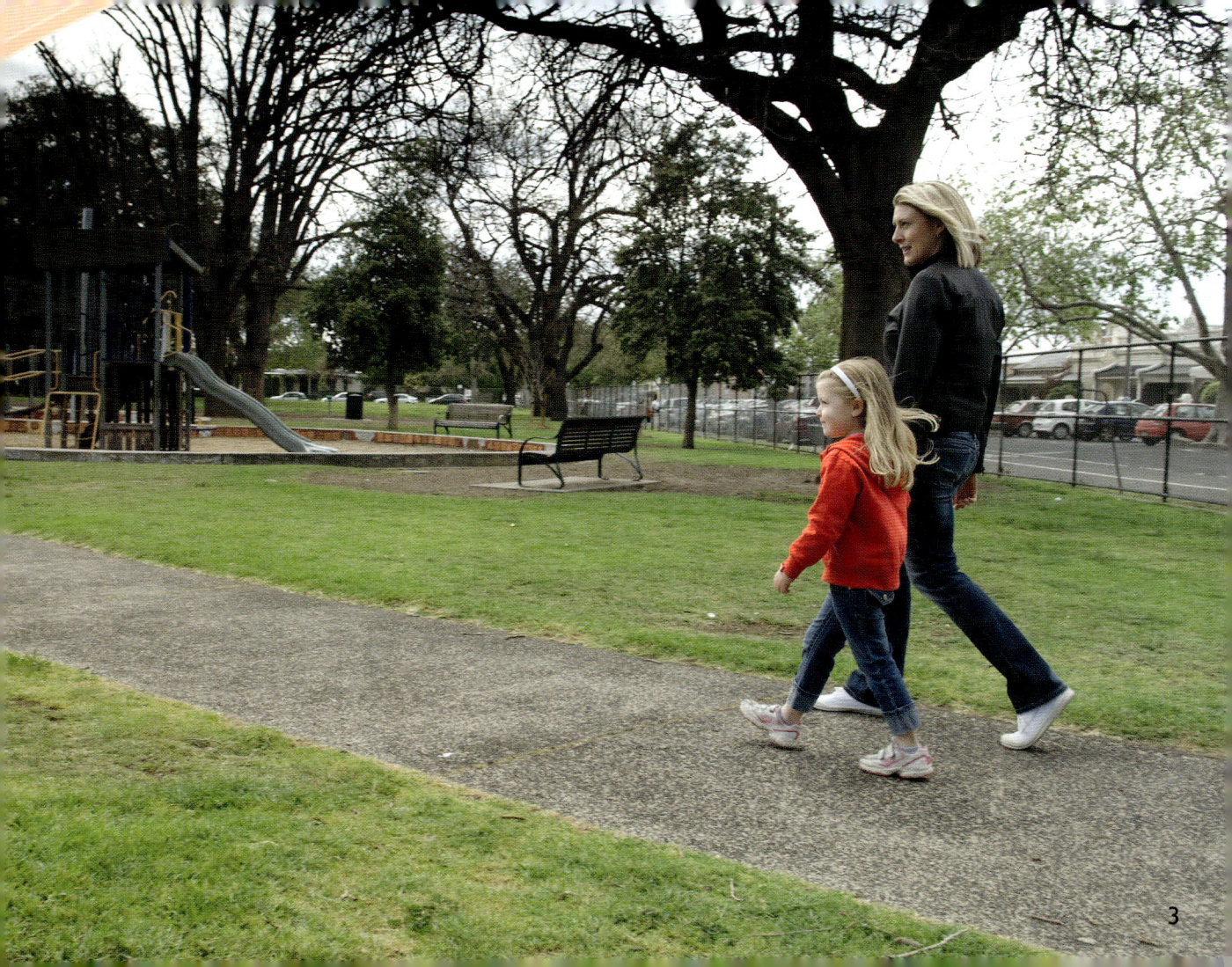

Mum and I went to the beach.

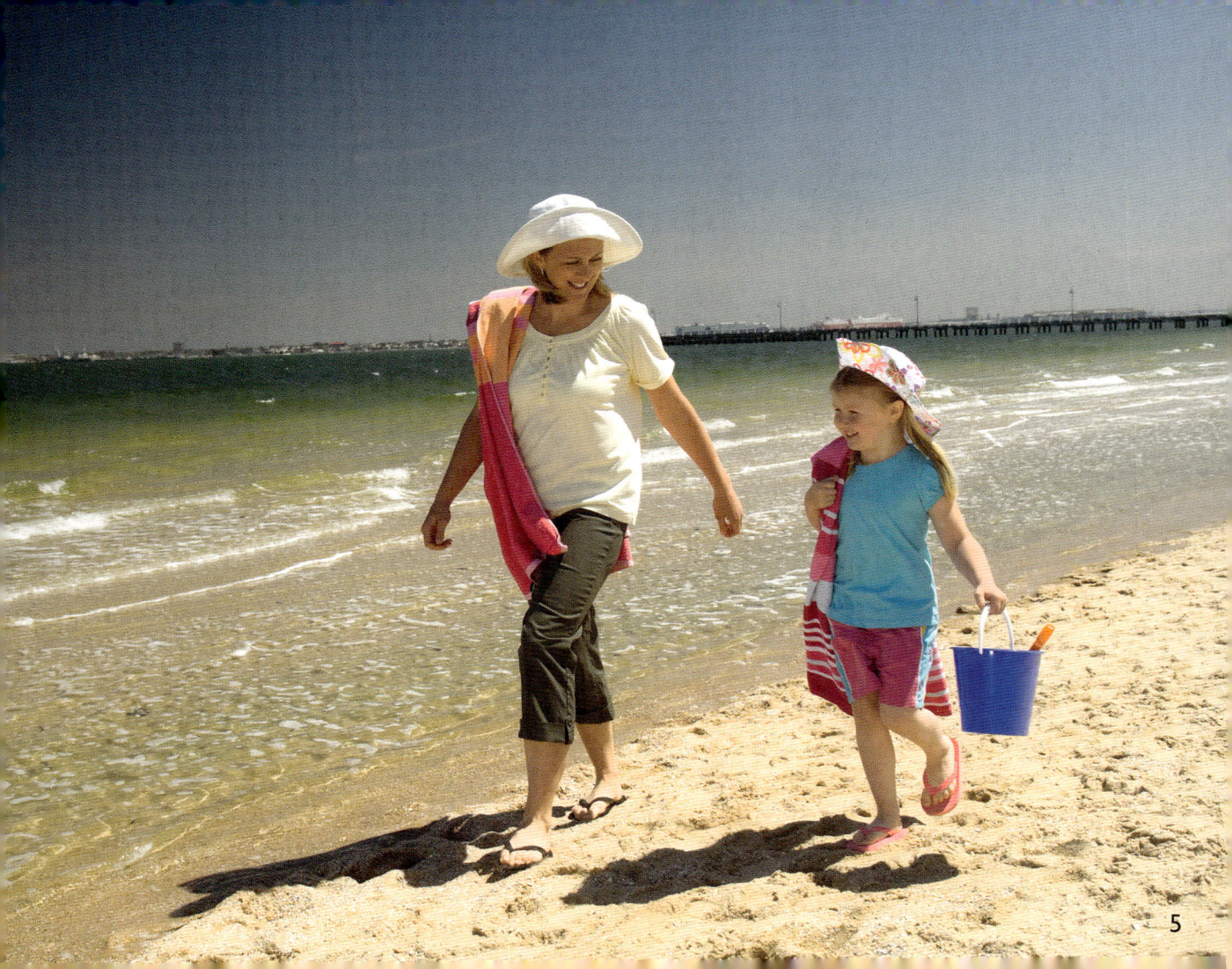

Mum and I
went to the shop.

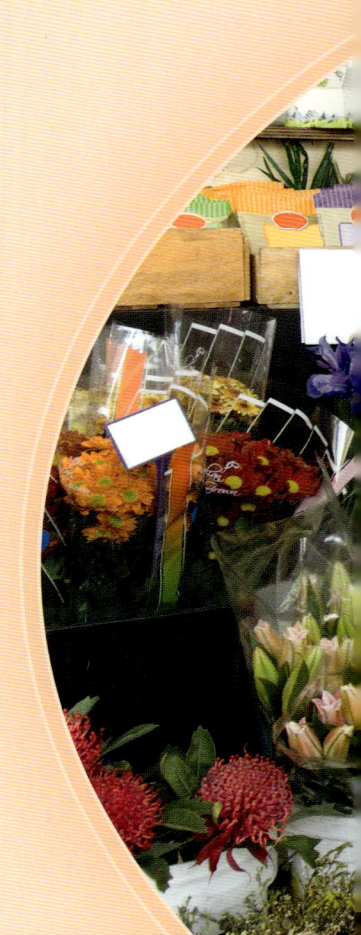

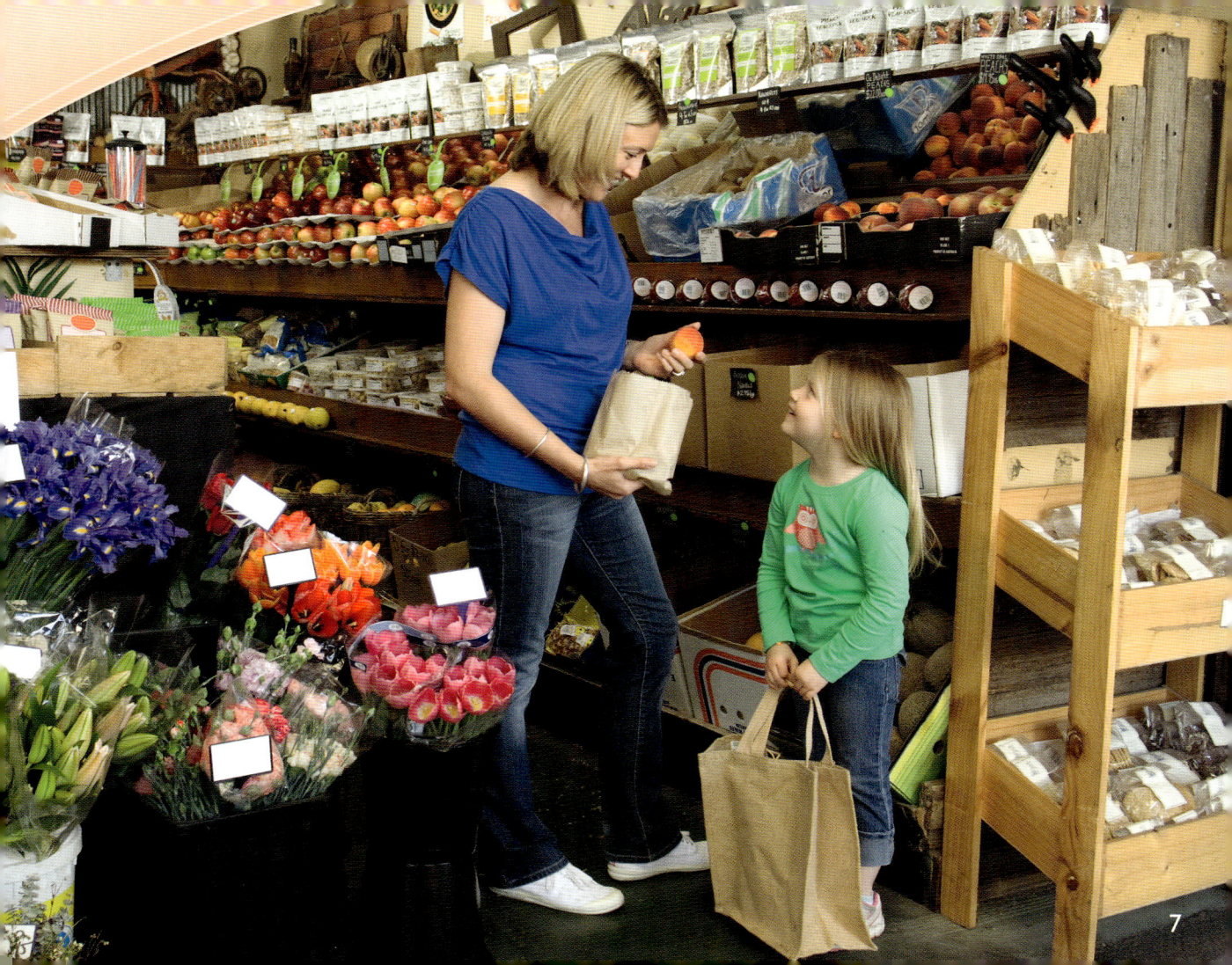

Mum and I
went to the movies.

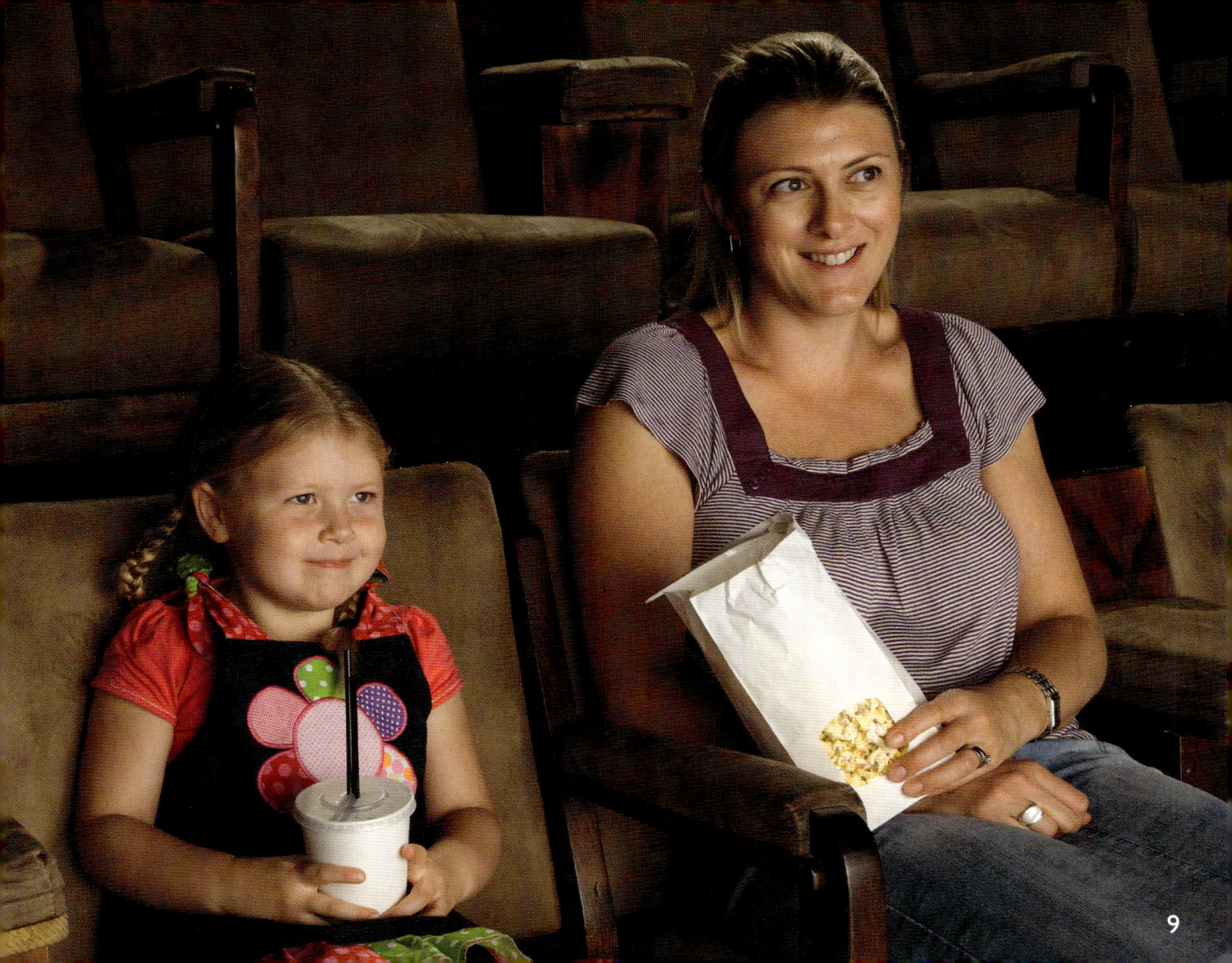

Mum and I
went to the pool.

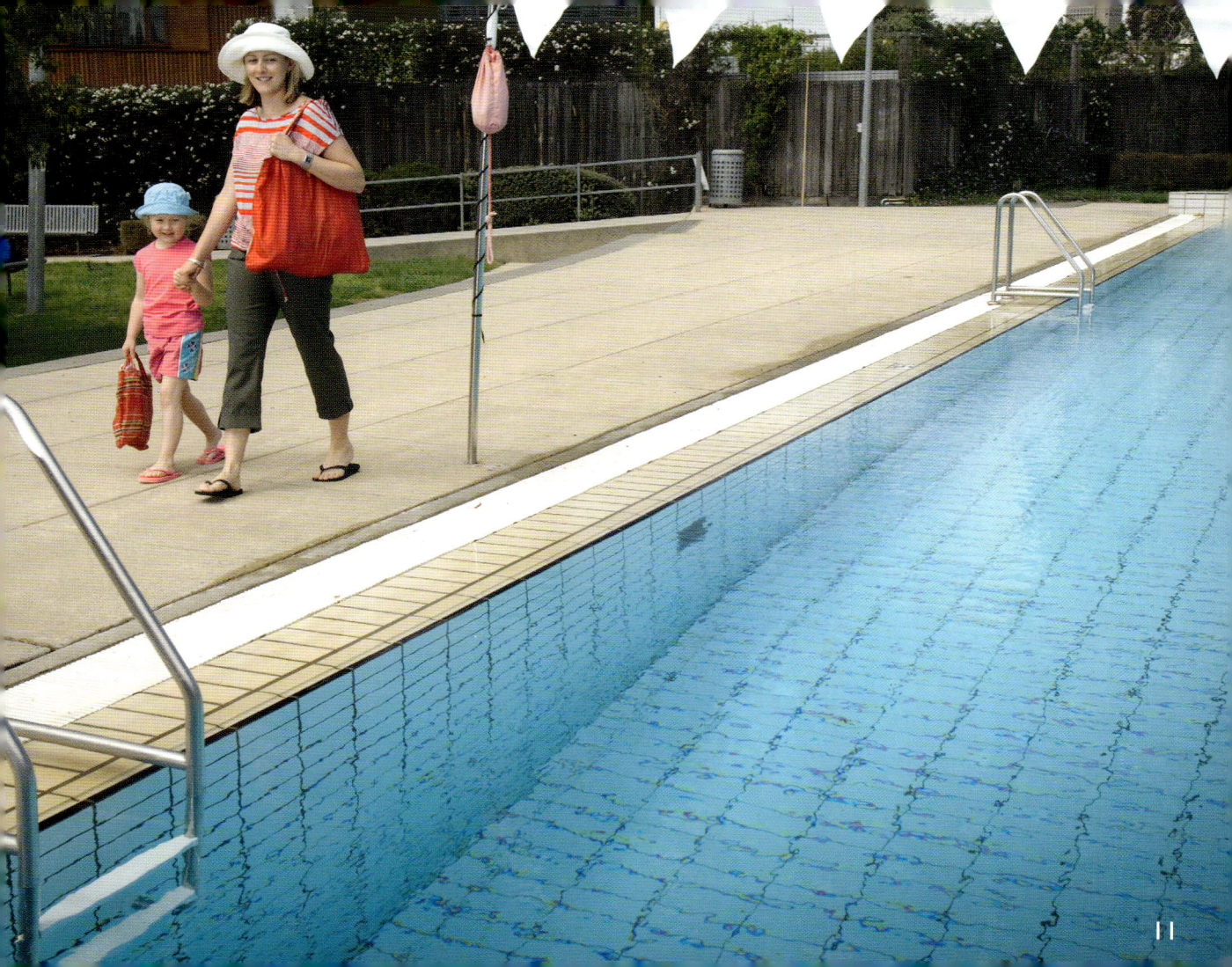

Mum and I
went to the zoo.

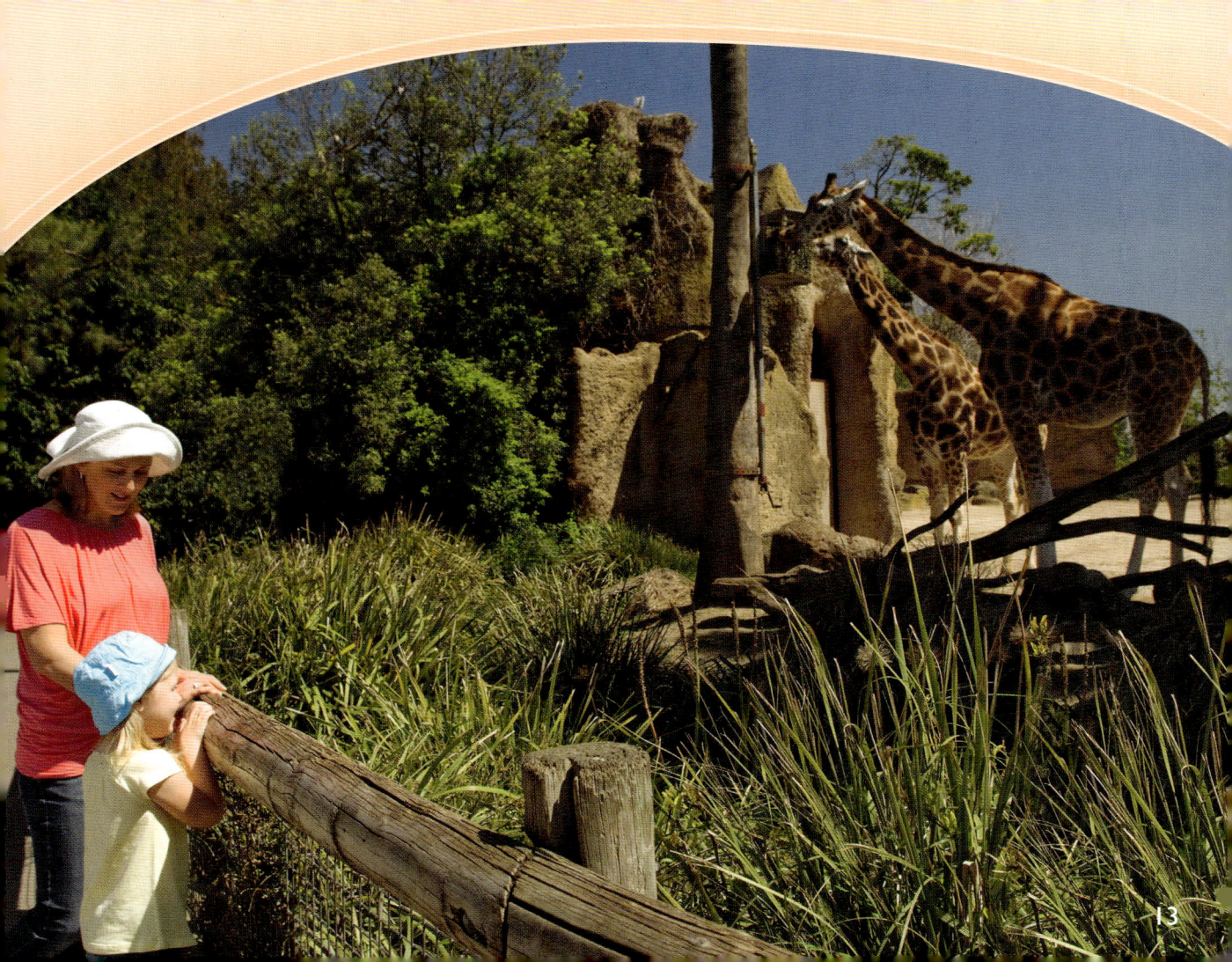

Mum and I
went to the library.

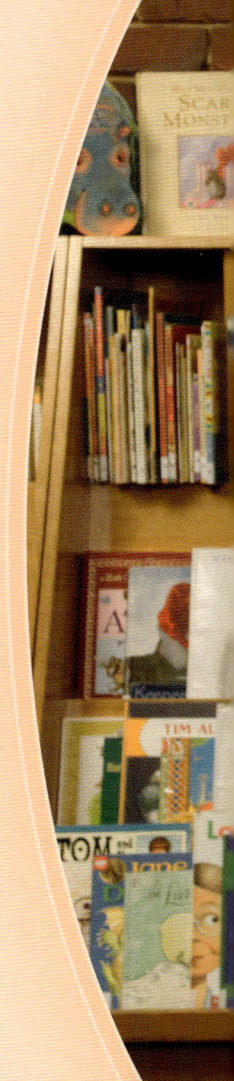

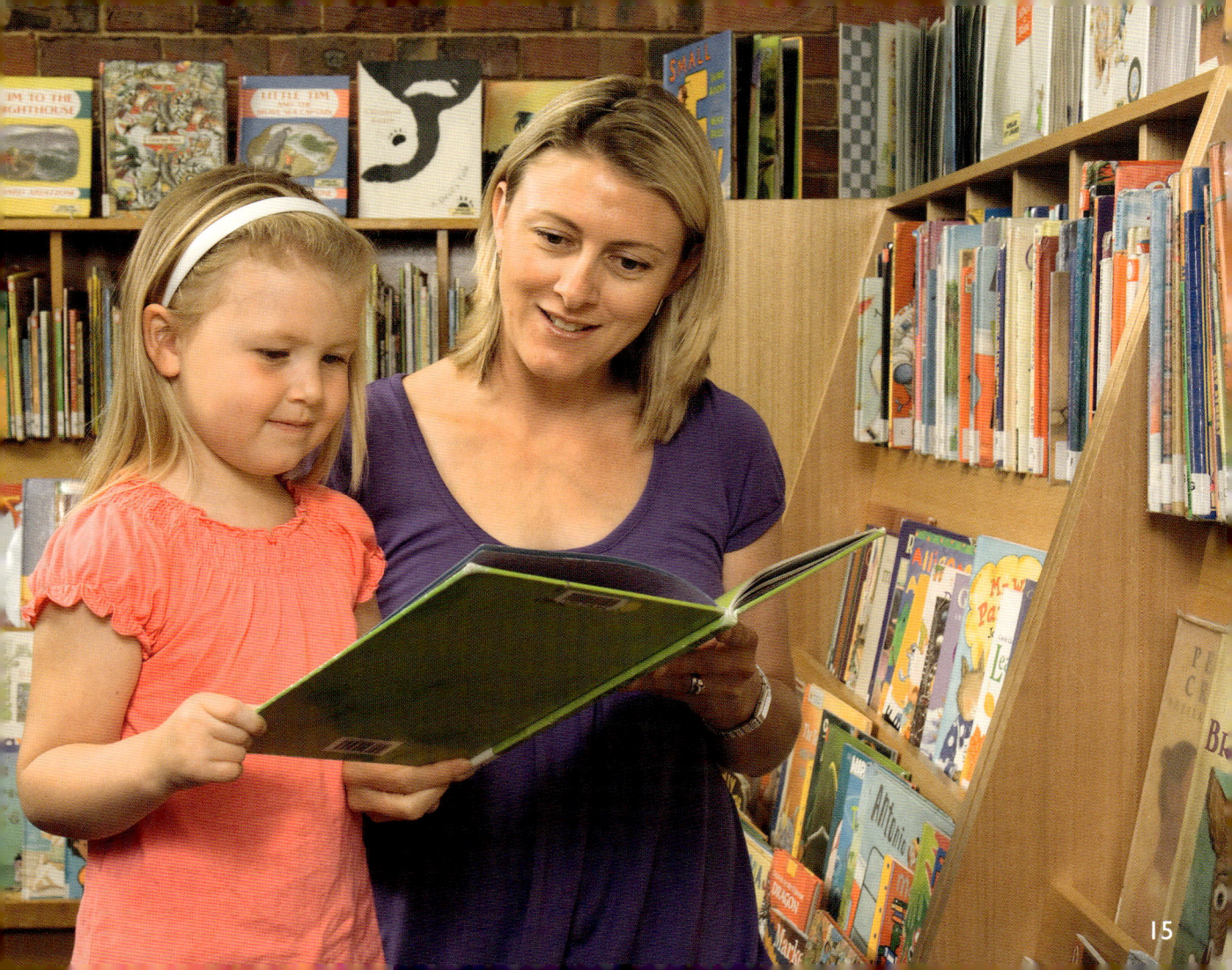

Mum and I went to the market.

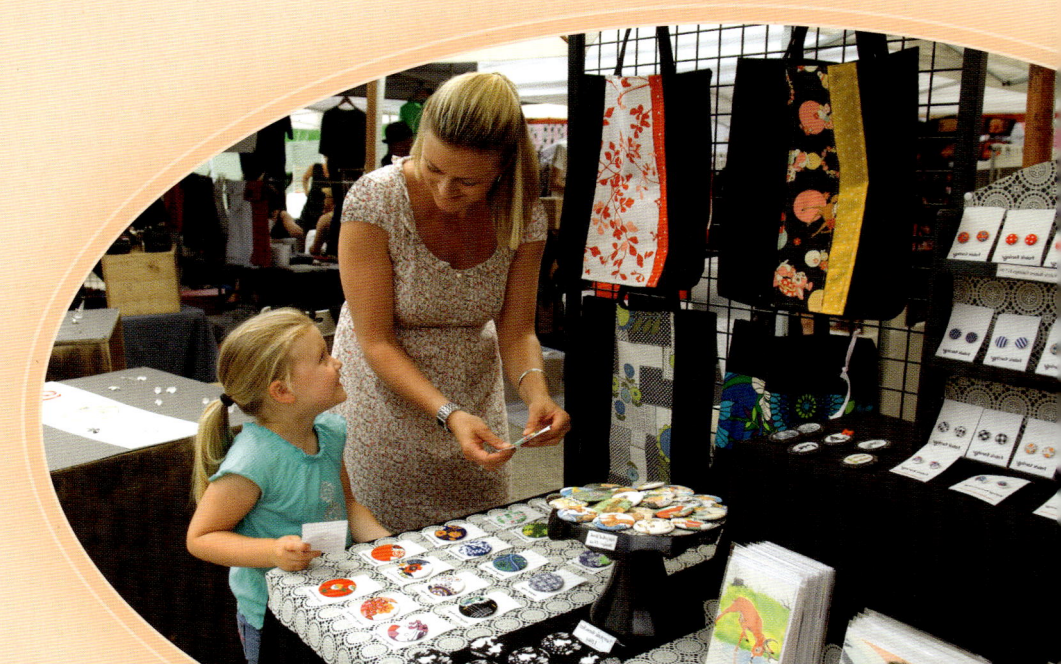